William Bolcom/Arnold Weinstein

Cabaret Songs

Volumes 3 and 4

for medium voice and piano

CONTENTS

Third Edition

ISBN 0-7935-9116-3

EDWARD B. MARKS MUSIC COMPANY / EXCLUSIVELY DISTRIBUTED BY HAL•LEONARD® CORPORATION

7777 W. BLUEMOUND RD. P.O. BOX 13819 MILWAUKEE, WI 53213

Although **Cabaret Songs** were written for Joan Morris, technically a mezzo-soprano, these songs are intended to be sung in a diseur or diseuse tessitura, that is, principally using the lower half of the vocal range. Volumes 3 and 4 have a lower tessitura than the first two volumes:

 (the inner notes represent the principally-used range, the outer the rarely-used extremes)

This does not mean the singer should use chest tone exclusively! A more speaking tone is recommended in order to give the words equal value to the notes. (Bear the above in mind when deciding what transposition may be necessary.)

These songs are not written with operatic voice-classifications in mind, although they are performable by the trained voice and have often been so. Thus they can be fairly efficacious training in theater-style performance for voice students.

W.B.

N.B. - Accidentals apply only throughout a beamed group:

but ♮♭♮. In music with a key signature, traditional practice is observed.

What Is Cabaret Song

First, what it is not. It is not, like these notes, For Musicians Only. No piano tinkling unmerrily away out for an evening of no fun, especially for the words whose un-accented syllables are deftly fudged by accented accompaniment. As Lester Young said, "Play the words."

But what is cabaret song? Is it the long letter to the *Sad-Eyed Lady of the Lowlands* sung by sad Dylan or his commercial for psychedelics, *Tambourine Man,* or the John Wesley Harding dirge? Unh unh, them's western ballads sung in saloons of the Pecos, not in cabarets, though Jacques Levy's lyrics to Dylan's hymn *Durango* saunter easily into the cabaret spot.

Dylan's partners, the Beats, don't sit too well either in the cabaret's dopeless smoke. Ginsberg's blues remain cantorial, stoned. Maybe Kerouac's hip haiku joined Stan Getz in a successful debut of improvisational lieder that could be listened to in a kind of club. Jazz and poetry spent a lot of time hanging out in bars, but jazz and poems do not generally a cabaret song make. Fran Landesman is the huge exception, supernally talented writer of *Spring Can Really Hang You Up the Most,* to be hoarsely incanted in the dark to all the Sad Young Men at the bar.

Cabaret stuff cannot be electrified to an audience of teary old timers at the Palace or the kids at the Palladium nor yet to Felt Forum throngs. Maybe in a small concert hall but not really; that's more an experience brought about by the heartbreaking wear and tear of cabaret life on its ill-paid performers who need the occasional lucrative airing.

So what are we left with? Well, *aimez-vous* Poulenc setting Apollinaire's *Hôtel,* not wanting *travailler* but *fumer?* What about García Lorca's *Malagueña,* in which Death "enters and exits/in the tavern," like an O'Neill whore, sung in the long lines of flamenco? Or the Italian *Stornelli* sung table to table by wandering improvisors in Rome and Florence?

Despite Virgil Thomson's accusation that British ballads are ungainly, the snippy maestro and master critic might agree that certain poets certainly qualify as makers of the soft-sung poem that lends itself to cabaret rendering: Shakespeare, Jonson, Donne, Campion, Sydney, Blake. And Dryden gave Purcell plenty to sing about in the key of cabaret.

But it is in Germany that the rhinestone mantle of cabaret is worn most comfortably. Out of the Viennese café tradition that gave birth to Schubert's pop tunes, lieder in English, came the line from Oscar Straus to Brecht-Weill. Along the way, around the turn of our century, Schoenberg took time out from copying operetta scores to write a few dozen items called *Brettl-Lieder* — cabaret songs. (If you're lucky enough to find the record of Marni Nixon singing these you may be surprised.)

Brecht and Weill, vowing to "write for today, to hell with posterity," produced their immortal numbers under national conditions of stress, adumbrated in the stridency of their sound and image. The Brecht-Weill lyric rasping was played in all the Berlin clubs and has been played in all the theaters of the western world ever since; played and played since those fearful times because they wrote for that "today" that comes around again and again.

Cabaret likes such ideas. It was ears-on education for a Germany with an education limited to the few, and (even to those educated few) cabaret songs told much of what journalism left out. But the facts and notions taught in the sawdust classrooms of cabaret nite-life were collaged of poetry and flagrancy — not unlike the expressionist cinema of the day, nor the pre-postmodernism of Kurt Schwitters. And the lessons preached by Brecht of the preacher's family and the cantorial Weill were the doctrines of Einstein, Freud and Marx decked out in the lipstick and mascara of cabaret.

The idea of Ideas as kissing cousins of popular song might make some sense if you remember that Bacon, Harvey and Newton, Galileo and Copernicus were contemporaries of the same Elizabethan songmakers who gave us the innovations of sound and seriousness that characterize the lyric output of Dowland, Morley, Blow, Byrd. And though there were no cabarets at the time, there were taverns and street-corners and theaters where the small sound prevailed; folk and gentility met in the ballads that sang the news of the day.

The courtly and the popular were blended as early as the 15th century and wandered together with the *chansonniers* through the Renaissance. In *Marriage à la Mode* Dryden talks of notions "sung in cabarets," and Pepys in his diary (also of the 17th century) records walls that read *"Dieu te regarde"* in the French cabarets. So it seems that cabarets favored political salt and amatory sult back then too.

In our era Kaufman had a cabaret talent until it was gentrified by Moss Hart. Then the two emulated the courtly in their exclusion of the popular rawness and genius Kaufman had shown in his absurdist

works 30 years before Absurdity. In our country Marc Blitzstein was solidly dedicated enough to have devoted serious musical energy to Saying Something. When asked why he tended to deploy his Schoenbergian background to sing of the unions, he answered, "Nothing is too good for the proletarian."

But the most daring moment in the history of cabaret occurred in Zurich in February 1916. On that day Dada was born; in the chintzy sleazy unartistic unintellectual atmosphere of the Cabaret Voltaire, the movement that was to transform modern art and lay the groundwork for post-modernism was announced by a reading by Tristan Tzara, followed by "performance art" by Arp and Kandinsky, lyrics by Wedekind, Morgenstern, Apollinaire, Marinetti, Cendrars. Designs by Modigliani, Picasso. Simultaneous reading of three poems "showing the struggle of the vox humana with . . . a universe of destruction whose noise is inescapable." (Hugo Ball's Diary).

An intellectually starved America, coming out of its long Puritanical fast, welcomed the new imports. Cabaret quality writing moved off the floor and onto the stage, where the '20s saw Rice's *Adding Machine* and Sophie Treadwell's *Machinal,* a kind of living newspaper that happened to star Clark Gable; in the '30s Rome's *Pins and Needles,* Blitzstein's *The Cradle Will Rock,* Weill's *Johnny Johnson* all had the episodic, collagistic approach characteristic of cabaret. Even *Our Town* has the spare, loose quality of revue, with the cohesiveness of real theme that makes it cabaretlike in form.

In England Auden had begun his campaign against the uncouth refinement of political rhetoric:

Stop all the clocks, cut off the telephone...
Let airplanes circle mourning overhead
Scribbling on the sky the message HE IS DEAD.
Put crepe bows round the necks of the public doves.
Let the traffic policemen wear black cotton gloves.

Clear and simple, but demanding that imagistic attention characteristic of the cabaret experience. Auden also wrote such wry songs (to Britten's delicious music) as *Tell Me the Truth About Love:*

Is it prickly to touch as a hedge is
Or soft as eiderdown fluff,
Is it sharp or smooth at the edges.
O tell me the truth about love.

which, apart from the ironic (we hope) fluff/love rhyme, is like afterhours Cole Porter. But even the love songs of cabaret have a conspiratorial quality.

Thus, passing to the left, the Living Theater, the Open Theater, Caffé Cino; to the right, Bway and, off-right, Off-Bway; in between was the Artist Theater (Koch, O'Hara, Ashbery accompanied by New York painters rather than musicians). And in some political bunker of their own architecting, a couple of writers met and wrote the songs on this album.

Norse-American William Bolcom the composer studied with Roethke the poet, and before that, his feet barely hitting the pedals, Bill had played for the vaudeville shows passing through Seattle with such songs in the repertory as *Best Damn Thing Am Lamb Lamb Lamb.* Milhaud found Bill and brought him back alive to highbrow music, though he never lost his lowbrow soul (neither did Milhaud). Operas later, we wrote these songs as a cabaret in themselves, no production "values" to worry about. The scene is the piano, the cast is the singer, in this case Joan Morris, who inspired us with her subtle intimations of Exactly What She Wanted. We hope she got it. Nobody defines better than she this elusive form of theater-poetry-lieder-pop-tavernacular prayer called cabaret song.

—*ARNOLD WEINSTEIN*

In addition to the *Cabaret Songs,* William Bolcom and Arnold Weinstein have collaborated on several projects, including the underground classic *Dynamite Tonite,* an opera for actors. Among Mr. Bolcom's recent compositions is a full-evening setting of William Blake's *Songs of Innocence and of Experience,* for soloists, choruses and expanded orchestra, which was premiered in January 1984 by Dennis Russell Davies conducting the Stuttgart Opera. Mr. Weinstein has written librettos for David Amram, Tony Greco, Oliver Lake, Laurence Rosenthal, William Russo and Henry Threadgill; his plays include *Red Eye of Love,* and *Metamorphoses* for Paul Sills' Story Theater. He is also a professor in the English department at Columbia University.

VOLUME THREE The Total Stranger in the Garden

Poem by **Arnold Weinstein**

Music by **William Bolcom**

Lyrics under the vocal line:

Sit- ting a- cross the ta - ble In the gar - den of our gar- den a - part - ment I stared at the pa - per ___ my hus- band was read - ing And I said to him: You're a stran - ger A to - tal stran - ger

You to - tal stran - ger _ You stran - ger, you!

Then he low - ered the pa - per And I

saw it was not my hus - band But a to - tal stran - ger A

to - tal stran - ger ____ who said to me:

Slow (♩=c.60)

"I am a kind of ho-bo of space

Try-ing to find a mask ___ to e-rase The mask be-hind The

non rit.

mask be-hind The mask be-hind The face."

January 27, 1978 Ann Arbor

Love in the Thirties

Poem by **Arnold Weinstein**

Music by **William Bolcom**

we can't af - ford it.

Dad,

I saw the dev - il on the fi - re es - cape,

long point - ed pus - sy ears. _____ What kind of dev - il is

that, kid? __ No tail, no horns.

we'll let you know, you'll see __

Dad, how __ will I see? __

You'll see __ "by the light of your sil - ver - y heart."

I'm talk-ing sci-ence now, kid. Dad,

Slow

Thius King of Orf

Poem by **Arnold Weinstein**

Music by **William Bolcom**

Free, not slow

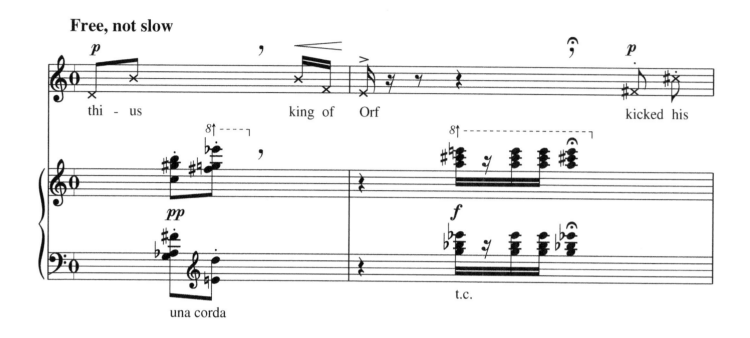

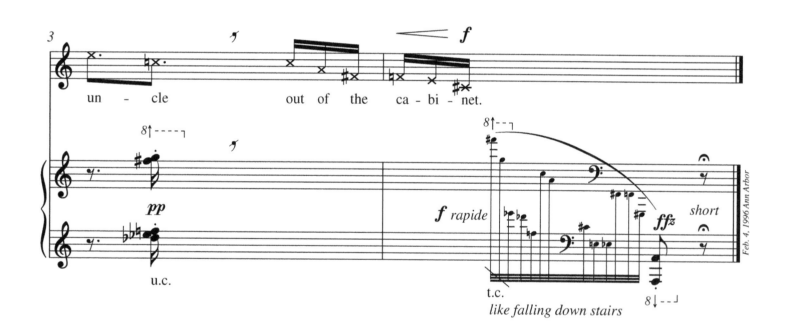

Miracle Song

Poem by **Arnold Weinstein**

Music by **William Bolcom**

* *This should give a muted, harsh sound. Also see meas. 11, 15, 65, and 68.*

Death in the pa - per

death on the phone

poco rit.

death a - cross a crowd - ed

a tempo

clo - set _____ death on the street ev - 'ry

rit.

third friend you meet: "Hel- lo, so what else is

Satisfaction

Poem by **Arnold Weinstein**

Music by **William Bolcom**

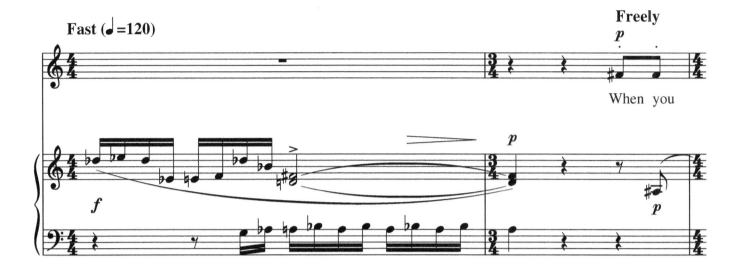

When you

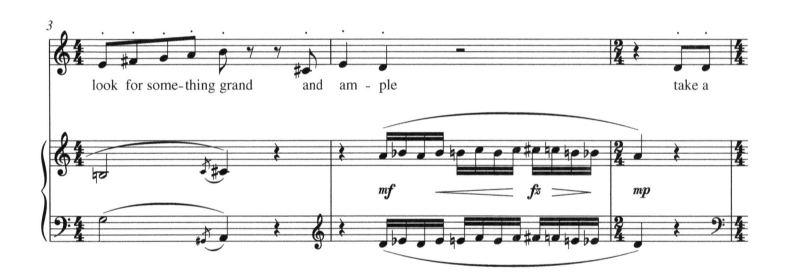

look for some-thing grand and am - ple   take a

bee   for a   sam-ple: sits a se-cond on a rose __

July 7, 1984 Ann Arbor

for Dave Frishberg

Radical Sally

Poem by **Arnold Weinstein**   *Music by* **William Bolcom**

Bright (♩=112 or slower), in word-jazz style

She was al - ways there, al - ways there, no mat - ter where, she was there. At Brad-ley's Bar (be-fore it was a res-tau-rant and it was just a bar), Rad-i-cal Sal-ly __ look-ing for a cause __ and we'd walk in __ And there she'd be __

star - ing like a dead tree at you at me es - pec - ial - ly

you.

And the Five Spot: Monk and Trane and La -

- dy Day sit - tin' in

(loud crowd hushed) And there in the gloom _____

like muted trumpets

mf

pp

sempre

ff dim.

Rad - i - cal

Sal - ly ___ sip - pin' and grin - nin' ___ in _

poco cresc.

_____ the ap - plause _____ Grin - nin' at some - thing some -

p

slower and slower

sip - ping mar - ga - ri - tas _____ with a look of I knew you

when _____ (when did she know?) _____

Adagio

Tempo I

And the day in Big Sur _

She was at Ne - pen - the _

March 6, 1996 Ann Arbor

VOLUME FOUR

VOLUME FOUR

for Barbara Harris

Angels Are the Highest Form of Virtue

Poem by **Arnold Weinstein**

Music by **William Bolcom**

mar-tyrs glad-ly die and die a - gain   But the birds,   the birds   I

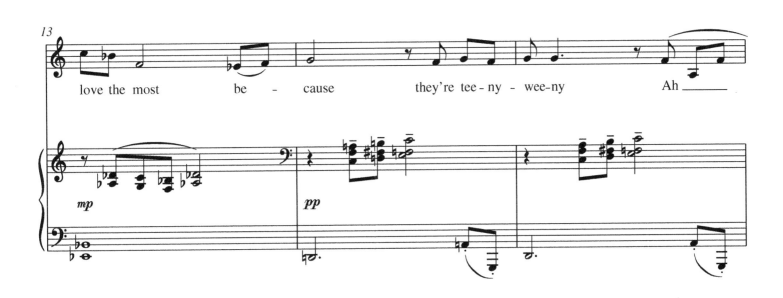

love the most   be - cause   they're tee-ny - wee-ny   Ah

rit.   **Very slow**

Ah   espr. e mist.

March 7, 1996. Rev. from 1963

Poet Pal of Mine

Poem by **Arnold Weinstein**

Music by **William Bolcom**

Lively (♩=c.60)

Po-et pal of mine! _____ Dead but so what. Your words, Your verse, So strik - ing! _____ Who can ev - er for - get The son - net that be - gan _____ "Oh Rus - sian

March 13, 1996 Ann Arbor

Can't Sleep

Poem by **Arnold Weinstein**

Music by **William Bolcom**

Like a lullaby (♩=c.66)

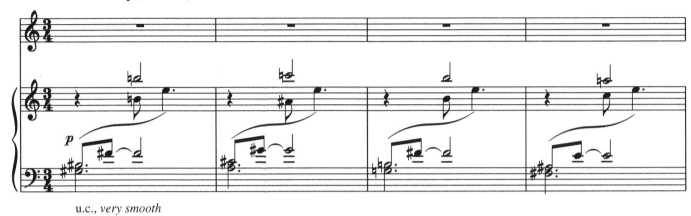

u.c., *very smooth*

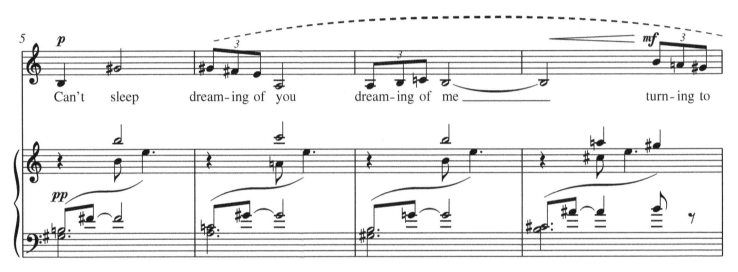

Can't sleep dream-ing of you dream-ing of me _____ turn-ing to

you wok-en by me. _____

t.c., *slowly*

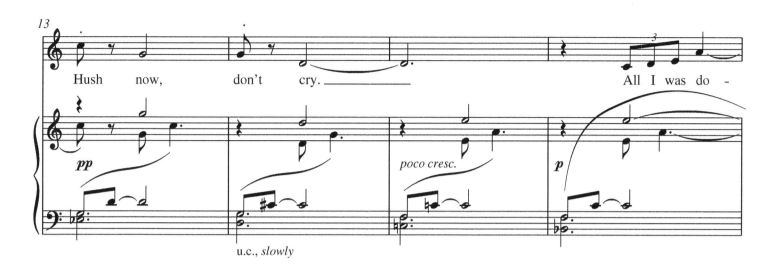

Hush now, don't cry. _____ All I was do-

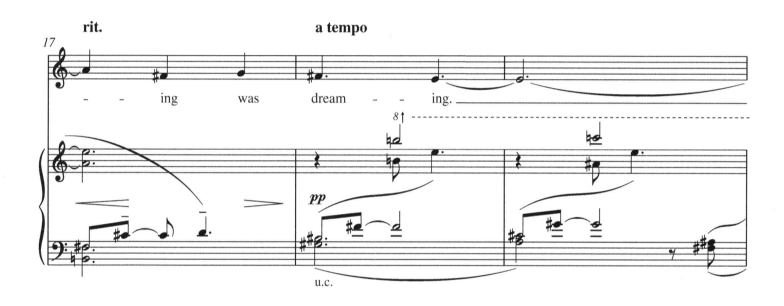

rit. a tempo

- - ing was dream - ing. _____

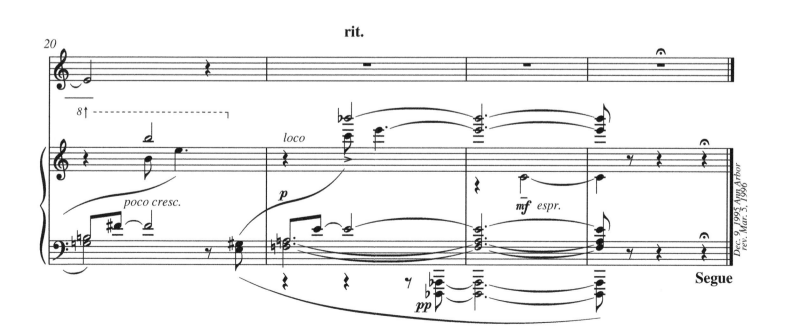

rit.

Segue

At the Last Lousy Moments of Love

Poem by **Arnold Weinstein**

Music by **William Bolcom**

* can be used throughout if desired

** This chord is optional if the song follows directly from <u>Can't Sleep</u>.

November 3, 1995 Ann Arbor

Arnold Weinstein and William Bolcom
© Nancy Lee Katz 1999

*William Bolcom, Joan Morris, and Arnold Weinstein
at the Chelsea Hotel, New York City*

Lady Luck

Poem by **Arnold Weinstein**

Music by **William Bolcom**

April 25, 1996 NYC

Blue

Poem by **Arnold Weinstein**

Music by **William Bolcom**

and now all I want to do my heart is sit real

still with you. Af - ter all that screech-ing talk - ing fast and

slow - ing down on - ly now and then to reach you when you'd

let me know I knew that what I preach is none too true

34

that's why all I   want   to do   my heart   is   sit   real   still   with

♩=66, more rhythmic, not too fast

38   *cresc.*

you.   (Cause I   do know this a- bout peo-ple   and I DONT mean some:

pp   *cresc.*

                                                                                      sim.

41   *poco a poco*   *f*   *p*

aw - f 'ly smart peo-ple   are   of - ten aw-ful   dumb!   Aren't we?   We

poco a poco   *f > p*

poco accel.

44

just   don't   re - al - ize ___   that   be - hind   the   eyes,   be -

cresc.

March 17, 1996 Ann Arbor

America's favorite book of Cabaret Songs
featuring "Black Max" and "Amor"

William Bolcom/Arnold Weinstein

CABARET SONGS

Volumes 1 and 2

for medium voice and piano

CONTENTS